YOUR KNOWLEDGE HAS VALUE

Bibliographic information published by the German National Library:

The German National Library lists this publication in the National Bibliography; detailed bibliographic data are available on the Internet at http://dnb.dnb.de .

Imprint:

Copyright © 2017 GRIN Verlag, Open Publishing GmbH
Print and binding: Books on Demand GmbH, Norderstedt Germany
ISBN: 9783668607484

This book at GRIN:

https://www.grin.com/document/386600

Anonym

A Comparative Analysis of the Governments of the United States of America and Germany and their Historical Development

GRIN Publishing

GRIN - Your knowledge has value

Since its foundation in 1998, GRIN has specialized in publishing academic texts by students, college teachers and other academics as e-book and printed book. The website www.grin.com is an ideal platform for presenting term papers, final papers, scientific essays, dissertations and specialist books.

Visit us on the internet:

http://www.grin.com/

http://www.facebook.com/grincom

http://www.twitter.com/grin_com

Thema:

A Comparative Analysis of the Governments of the United States of America and Germany and their Historical Development

Table of Contents

1 Introduction

With the presidential elections in the United States of America just behind us and the "Bundestagswahl" in Germany just ahead of us, the controversies and challenges surrounding both elections warrant a closer look at the similarities and differences of the governmental systems of both countries to gain insights into the future of German and U.S. politics.

1.1 Thesis Statement

Even though the President of the United States of America is more powerful than the German "Bundeskanzler", the governmental system of Germany is better because the German electoral system is more democratic than that of the United States, and the German people are better represented by the politicians they elect. Particularly, the German executive, which is made up of multiple institutions, is much better than the U.S. executive in the person of a president who has a lot of power and is able to single handily change important laws and rules of the nation.

1.2 Motivation

This Facharbeit about the governmental systems of the United States of America (USA) and Germany is a result of the author's interest in history and politics in combination with the requirement to select a topic relating to the USA. Furthermore, this topic is really interesting, as there were a lot of negative articles about the U.S. electoral system in the newspapers during the last U.S. presidential elections in November of 2016. The upcoming "Bundestagswahl" in Germany later in 2017[1] makes the topic even more relevant. This research report will compare the governmental systems of Germany and the USA, their electoral systems, and their historical development. The goal of the essay is to determine the advantages and disadvantages of a presidential system and a parliamentary democracy and to conclude which system is better for the citizens and gives them more political influence.

1.3 Methodology

The research for this Facharbeit is based on books borrowed from the library, interesting newspaper articles and a number of internet sources. The German and American governmental systems and their development have been widely researched, so there is no lack of suitable materials for the topic.

---

[1]"Bundestagswahl 2017." *Der Bundeswahlleiter.* Web. 27 Jan. 2017.

The first sections of this essay will provide an overview of the historical developments of the constitutions and governmental systems of each country, followed by a detailed description of each system. The information presented will mainly be out of books from the library. The following comparison of the political influence of the citizens and the influence of the governmental systems overall will also be based on sources available through the library, as well as on newspaper articles.

2 The governmental system of Germany

2.1 The historical development of the governmental system of Germany

After the end of the Second World War in 1945 and Germany's capitulation, the country was occupied and controlled by foreign nations[2]. This was the time when the founding process of today's "Bundesrepublik Deutschland" started[3]. The occupying powers had different objectives for their politics in Germany. For instance, exploiting the country through war reparations was the aim of Soviet Union. The Soviet occupied zone of Germany was considered as an extension of the Soviet Union[4]. The United States of America set democratization and denazification as their goals, while the United Kingdom had economic interests and promoted German self-administration[5]. France had the target to affiliate their area to their own country and delimitate it from Germany.

To supply the German population with food and re-establish schools and other public institutions, all occupying powers wanted to improve the administrative structure[6]. Gradually, two different developments occurred in Germany because the western powers had other political interests than the Soviet Union. This eventually resulted in two separate parts being established: The "Bundesrepublik Deutschland" (BRD) as a part of the western alliance system and the "Deutsche Demokratische Republik" (DDR) as part of the Soviet system[7].

Only the development of the BRD is relevant for the foundation of today´s governmental system of Germany. Because of that this will be shown in the following part of the text.

The BRD went through several developmental periods: The first period was in the 1950s when Germany experienced great economic prosperity[8]. A liberal and social market economy was made possible by a new constitution and the ambitious reconstruction politics supported by the western powers[9]. The division of responsibilities between local

[2]Würz, Markus. "Alliierte Besatzung." *Lebendiges Museum Online*. Web. 7 Feb. 2017.
[3]Hesse, Joachim Jens, and Thomas Ellwein. "Das Deutsche Regierungssystem: Ausgangsbedingungen Und Entwicklung." *Das Regierungssytem Der Bundesrepublik Deutschland*. 11.
[4]ibid. 12.
[5]Ibid. 12.
[6]"Die Ziele Der Alliierten 1945-1949." *Konrad Adenauer Stiftung*. Web. 10 Feb. 2017.
[7]Hesse, Joachim Jens, and Thomas Ellwein. "Das Deutsche Regierungssystem: Ausgangsbedingungen Und Entwicklung." *Das Regierungssytem Der Bundesrepublik Deutschland*. 13. Print.
[8]Kriwet, Hildegard. "Wirtschaftswunder." *Planet Wissen*. Web. 14 Feb. 2017.
[9]Hesse, Joachim Jens, and Thomas Ellwein. "Das Deutsche Regierungssystem: Ausgangsbedingungen Und Entwicklung." *Das Regierungssystem Der Bundesrepublik Deutschland*. 14.

communes, federal states and a federal government was established[10] and with the money from the economic success, about three million new flats were built to provide much needed housing for the German population[11].

The second period lasted from 1960 until 1968. During this time, the reconstruction in Western Germany came to its end[12]. Now that the basic needs of the people were satisfied, the focus of the population, especially the university students, claimed better participation in the political process. Student protests eventually resulted in a change at the federal government level[13]. The voters forced the party that had run the country for two decades – the "Christlich Demokratische Union Deutschlands" - into a grand coalition with the "Sozialdemokratische Partei Deutschlands"[14]. Overall, this second period resulted in increasing stability of the BRD as a country[15].

In the third period, which dates from 1969 until 1982[16], Germany invested most of its financial resources into improvements of the education system. This included compulsory education and a reform of the secondary education system[17]. The oil crisis of 1973 caused economic growth to stagnate, which in turn resulted in rising unemployment numbers[18]. Because the financial resources were depleted, there were no more reforms and Germany had to implement the energy saving law to deal with the energy crisis[19]. This law initially led to the formation of groups against the establishment[20], because the German citizens wanted to save the environment and protect themselves from the risk of nuclear power. Eventually, these groups founded a new political party: "Die Grünen"[21].

[10]"Historische Entwicklung Und Entstehung Der 16 Bundesländer." *Deutschland Ueberblick.de*. Web. 14 Feb. 2017.
[11]Hesse, Joachim Jens, and Thomas Ellwein. "Das Deutsche Regierungssystem: Ausgangsbedingungen Und Entwicklung." *Das Regierungssystem Der Bundesrepublik Deutschland*. 15.
[12]Heinz, Tobias. "Wiederaufbau Durch Ausländer – Türken Und Türkische Gastarbeiter in Deutschland." *Formelheinz*. Web. 14 Feb. 2017.
[13]Carrasco, Ines. "Studentenbewegung." *Planet Wissen*. Web. 10 Feb. 2017.
[14]Hesse, Joachim Jens, and Thomas Ellwein. "Das Deutsche Regierungssystem: Ausgangsbedingungen Und Entwicklung." *Das Regierungssystem Der Bundesrepublik Deutschland*. 16.
[15]Würz, Markus. "Geteiltes Deutschland." *Lebendiges Museum Deutschland*. Web. 14 Feb. 2017.
[16]Hesse, Joachim Jens, and Thomas Ellwein. "Das Deutsche Regierungssystem: Ausgangsbedingungen Und Entwicklung." *Das Regierungssystem Der Bundesrepublik Deutschland*. 16.
[17]"Bildungsexpansion Und Schulreform in Der Bundesrepublik." *Chroniknet*. Web. 14 Feb. 2017.
[18]Grünhagen, Jürgen. "Die Ölkrise 1973." *N-tv*. Web. 14 Feb. 2017.
[19]Hesse, Joachim Jens, and Thomas Ellwein. "Das Deutsche Regierungssystem: Ausgangsbedingungen Und Entwicklung." *Das Regierungssystem Der Bundesrepublik Deutschland*. 17.
[20]Fuchs, Hans Joachim. "Umwelt Und Nachhaltigkeit." *Konrad Adenauer Stiftung*. Web. 14 Feb. 2017.
[21]Hofmann, Rebecca. "Entstehung Der Grünen." *Planet Wissen*. Web. 7 Feb. 2017.

After the political system lost some authority in the 1970s, the next period started in 1982 with the new "Bundeskanzler" Helmut Kohl and ended with the German reunification in 1990. Chancellor Kohl reduced the unemployment rate, increased consumer confidence and stabilized the German economy[22]. In 1989, the eastern part of Germany (DDR) became politically unstable. Mass demonstrations led to the resignation of the SED-government[23] and after a new travel-law went into effect, the border between East and West Germany was opened on the 9th of November 1989[24]. In the "Zwei plus Vier"-contract, France, the United States of America, the United Kingdom and the Soviet Union agreed upon the reunification of East and West Germany, which officially was on the 3rd of October 1990[25]. Since then, the combined East and West Germany is also a member of European Union[26].

---

[22]Hesse, Joachim Jens, and Thomas Ellwein. "Das Deutsche Regierungssystem: Ausgangsbedingungen Und Entwicklung." *Das Regierungssystem Der Bundesrepublik Deutschland*. 18.

[23]"Demonstrationen in Der Ganzen DDR." *Jugendopposition*. Web. 7 Feb. 2017.

[24]Hemmerich, Lisa. "Das Folgenreichste Versehen Der DDR-Geschichte." *Spiegel Online*. Web. 7 Feb. 2017.

[25]Petschow, Annabelle. "Zwei-plus-Vier-Vertrag." *Lebendiges Museum Online*. Web. 7 Feb. 2017.

[26]"Erweiterung Der Europäischen Union." *Die Bundesregierung*. Web. 13 Feb. 2017.

2.2 The political system of Germany

The political system of Germany is divided into three levels of government[27]:

The communes, which are responsible for tasks like garbage service, oversight of building projects, fire prevention, disaster management, local public transport and sewage disposal,[28] are on the smallest level of the governmental system[29]. These local governments are responsible for small cities and villages. According to the German constitution, the communes have to manage themselves[30]. Moreover, they are part of the federal states ("Bundesländer") of Germany[31].

On the next level of government there are the federal states[32]. In Germany there are sixteen federal states and each of them has its own constitution[33]. The Germans differentiate between the eleven old federal states, which made up the "Bundesrepublik Deutschland" before 1990, and the five new federal states, which made up the territory of the "Deutsche Demokratische Republik" until 1990[34]. The old federal states are Baden-Württemberg, Bavaria, Berlin, Bremen, Hamburg, Hessen, Lower Saxony, North Rhine-Westphalia, Rhineland-Palatinate, Saarland and Schleswig-Holstein. The new "Bundesländer" are Brandenburg, Mecklenburg-Western Pomerania, Saxony, Saxony-Anhalt and Thuringia[35]. Moreover, the state government institutions have various names. For instance, in the city states of Hamburg and Bremen, the state government is called the "Senat". In Bavaria, the state government is called the "Staatsregierung"[36]. The heads of state government have different names as well. Bremen and Hamburg are led by the "Präsident des Senats" and Berlin is represented by the "Regierender Bürgermeister". All other federal states call their head of state the "Ministerpräsident"[37]. At the state level, only the members of the "Landesparlament" are directly elected by the citizens of each

---

[27]Straaß, Johannes, and Gerhard Krahl, Prof. Dr. "Das Politische System in Deutschland." *Politische Bildung Schwaben.* Web. 29 Jan. 2017.
[28]Was die Aufgaben der Kommunen sind." *Land Brandenburg.* Web. 29 Jan. 2017.
[29]Straaß, Johannes, and Gerhard Krahl, Prof. Dr. "Das Politische System in Deutschland." *Politische Bildung Schwaben.* Web. 29 Jan. 2017.
[30]"Gemeinden/Kommunale Selbstverwaltung." *Bundeszentrale für politische Bildung.* Web. 29 Jan. 2017.
[31]"Stellung der Kommunen im Staatsaufbau." *Niedersächsisches Ministerium für Inneres und Sport.* Web. 29 Jan. 2017.
[32]Straaß, Johannes, and Gerhard Krahl, Prof. Dr. "Das Politische System in Deutschland." *Politische Bildung Schwaben.* Web. 29 Jan. 2017.
[33]"Die Bundesländer Deutschlands." *Allgemeinwissen.com.* Web. 29 Jan. 2017.
[34]"Historische Entwicklung Und Entstehung Der 16 Bundesländer." *Deutschland Ueberblick.de.* Web. 14 Feb. 2017.
[35]"Was ist Föderalismus?" *Was ist Föderalismus?* Web. 29 Jan. 2017.
[36]"Land (Deutschland)." *Wikipedia.* Web. 29 Jan. 2017.
[37]"Die aktuellen Ministerpräsidenten der deutschen Bundesländer." *Wissen.de.* Web. 29 Jan. 2017.

state[38]. The head of state government, who is elected by the delegates of the "Landtag",[39] appoints the ministers[40] and together they form the state government which is responsible for the state administration and the law-making process.

The highest level of the governmental system of Germany, which is organized as a parliamentary democracy, is the federal government[41]. The federal government is divided into three branches: The legislative, the executive and the judicial branch[42]. These have to control each other and are represented by one or more political institutions. For instance, the "Bundestag" is associated with the legislative branch[43]. This German parliament is the center of the political system at the national level[44]. Currently, there are 598 lawmakers in the "Bundestag"[45] and their most important responsibilities include the enacting of new legislation and the monitoring of the federal government. They also exercise control over the federal budget and decide on deployments of the "Bundeswehr" to foreign countries[46]. Furthermore, the lawmakers are responsible for three important elections: The election of the "Bundeskanzler", the election of the "Bundespräsident" together with representatives of the "Landesparlamente" and the appointment of judges to the "Verfassungsgericht" together with the members of the "Bundesrat"[47]. The next election of the "Bundestag" is going to take place on the twenty-fourth of September 2017[48] and the last election of the "Bundespräsident" took place on the twelfth of February 2017[49].

Another political institution at the federal level is the "Bundesrat" which is also part of the legislative branch of government. It is called the parliament of "Bundesländerregierungen" because of the fact that all 69 members of the "Bundesrat" [50] are representatives of the

---

[38]"Landtagswahlen-Wofür eigentlich?" *RP Online*. Web. 29 Jan. 2017.
[39]"Wahlfunktion." *Landtag von Baden-Württemberg*. Web. 29 Jan. 2017.
[40]"Landtag wählt Dr. Dietmar Woidke zum Ministerpäsidenten und Ministerriege der neuen Landesregierung vereidigt." *Landtag Brandenburg*. Web. 29 Jan. 2017.
[41]Bognanni, Massimo. "Politisches System der Bundesrepublik Deutschland." *Zeit Online*. Web. 31 Jan. 2017.
[42]"Prinzip der Gewaltenteilung." *Der Bundestag*. Web. 31 Jan. 2017.
[43]Pötzsch, Horst. "Aufgaben des Bundestages." *Bundeszentrale für politische Bildung*. Web. 31 Jan. 2017.
[44]Seiffert, Jaenette. "Für das Volk-der deutsche Bundestag." *DW Made for minds*. Web. 31 Jan. 2017.
[45]"Wahl der Abgeordneten und Mandatsverteilung." *Deutscher Bundestag*. Web. 28 Jan. 2017.
[46]"Funktion und Aufgabe." *Deutscher Bundestag*. Web. 31 Jan. 2017.
[47]Ellermann, Viktoria, and Manuel Werder. "Der Deutsche Bundestag." *Abi-Box Politik-Wirtschaft: Demokratie und Sozialer Rechtsstaat*. 80.
[48]"Bundestagswahl 2017." *Der Bundeswahlleiter*. Web. 27 Jan. 2017.
[49]"Die Bundespräsidentenwahl 2017." *Landeszentrale für politische Bildung Baden-Württemberg*. Web. 31 Jan. 2017.
[50]"Mitglieder des Bundesrates." *Bundesrat*. Web. 31 Jan. 2017.

federal state governments of the sixteen "Bundesländer"[51]. The members of the "Bundesrat" are not elected by the German citizens and the number of representatives of each "Bundesland" depends on its population size[52]. The "Bundesratspräsident" represents the "Bundesrat"[53] and the position is currently held by Malu Dreyer, a member of the "Sozialdemokratische Partei Deutschland"[54]. The "Bundesratspräsident" is elected by the members of the "Bundesrat" every year on the first of November[55].

German legislation is always based on the "Grundgesetzbuch" and is the responsibility of the legislative institutions mentioned above[56]. Some laws about education, water supply and hunting are made by the "Landtage" at the state level, but all other laws are made by the "Bundestag" and the "Bundesrat" at the national level[57]. A draft law about new regulations or changes to existing legislation can be suggested by the "Bundesrat", the "Bundestag", or the "Bundesregierung". The "Bundestag" will discuss any new law proposal three times. At the end of the third reading, all members vote on it. To pass a new law, at least 50 percent of the members of the "Bundestag" have to vote in favor of it. Once a law has been passed by the "Bundestag", the "Bundesrat" also has to pass it before it goes into effect with the signature of the "Bundespräsident"[58].

The executive branch of government is the political institution of the "Bundesregierung". It includes the "Bundeskanzlerin", currently Angela Merkel, and her cabinet of ministers[59].

A judicial institution is the "Bundesverfassungsgericht" which has to pay attention on compliance with all legislation. If there is a problem between two governmental bodies it will resolve the conflict and in special cases it can forbid the work of a party in Germany[60].

[51]Ellermann, Viktoria, and Manuel Werder. "Der Bundesrat." *Abi-Box Politik-Wirtschaft: Demokratie und Sozialer Rechtsstaat.* 84.
[52]Ellermann, Viktoria, and Manuel Werder. "Die Bundesregierung." *Abi-Box Politik-Wirtschaft: Demokratie und Sozialer Rechtsstaat.* 85.
[53]"Präsidentin und Präsidium." *Bundesrat.* Web. 31 Jan. 2017.
[54]"Bundespräsidentin Malu Dreyer." *Bundesrat.* Web. 31 Jan. 2017.
[55]"Präsidentin und Präsidium." *Bundesrat.* Web. 31 Jan. 2017.
[56]Ellermann, Viktoria, and Manuel Werder. "Das Gesetzgebungsverfahren auf einen Blick." *Abi-Box Politik-Wirtschaft: Demokratie und Sozialer Rechtsstaat.* 81.
[57]"Die Gesetzgebung des Bundes." *Deutscher Bundestag.* Web. 31 Jan. 2017.
[58]Ellermann, Viktoria, and Manuel Werder. "Das Gesetzgebungsverfahren auf einen Blick." *Abi-Box Politik-Wirtschaft: Demokratie und Sozialer Rechtsstaat.* 81.
[59]Thurich, Eckart. "Bundesregierung." *Bundeszentrale Für Politische Bildung.* Web. 13 Feb. 2017.
[60]Ellermann, Viktoria, and Manuel Werder. "Das Bundesverfassungsgericht." *Abi-Box Politik-Wirtschaft: Demokratie Und Sozialer Rechtsstaat.* 87. Print.

2.2.1 The electoral system of Germany

In Germany, the citizens are able to elect the members of the "Bundestag", the members of the "Landtage" and the governments of the communes[61]. Each person who is at least eighteen years old, owns a German passport, has lived in Germany for more than three months and is in the electoral register[62] has the right to vote and the right to be elected[63]. However, in some federal states like Hamburg and Brandenburg, citizens who are sixteen years old already have the right to vote for the members of the "Länderparlamente" and the governments of the communes. The right to run for political office is only for people who are at least eighteen years old[64].

The election of the "Bundestag" takes place every four years. There were eighteen legislative periods since the German federal government was established[65] and the next election will take place on the twenty-fourth of September 2017[66]. The majority of the "Länderparlamente" are elected every five years by the citizens. Only in Bremen, the elections take place every four years[67]. Moreover, the majority of the elections of the commune governments are also every five years. Citizens of Bremen elect the local commune governments every four years. The Free State of Bavaria holds elections every six years[68].

According to the thirty-eighth paragraph of the German constitution, every political election in Germany has to be free, general, secret, equal and direct[69].

The elections of the "Bundestag" are based on the personal proportional representation model. This is a combination of the majority voting system and the proportional representation. Each voter in a "Bundestag"-election has two votes[70]. The first vote is for a particular politician from the voter's election district and the outcome is based on the majority voting system. In addition, the voters have the opportunity to elect a political party with their second vote which is tallied based on the proportional representation. Depending on how many votes a party receives, more politicians from this party will get

---

[61]"Welche Wahlen gibt es?" *Einmischen, Mitmischen. Politik für alle!* Web. 27 Jan. 2017.
[62]"Bundestagswahlen 2013." *Landeszentrale für politische Bildung Baden-Württenberg.* Web. 27 Jan. 2017.
[63]"Wahlrecht." *Rechtslexikon.net.* Web. 27 Jan. 2017.
[64]Zicht, Wilko. "Landtagswahlrecht." *Wahlrecht.* Web. 27 Jan. 2017.
[65]"Die bisherigen Wahlperioden des Bundestages." *Kürschners Politikkontakte.* Web. 27 Jan. 2017.
[66]"Bundestagswahl 2017." *Der Bundeswahlleiter.* Web. 27 Jan. 2017.
[67]Zicht, Wilko. "Landtagswahlrecht." *Wahlrecht.* Web. 27 Jan. 2017.
[68]Zicht, Wilko. "Komunalwahlrecht." *Wahlrecht.* Web. 28 Jan. 2017.
[69]"So funktionieren Wahlen: Allgemein, unmittelbar, frei, gleich und geheim." *Mach's ab 16! in Brandenburg.* Web. 28 Jan. 2017.
[70]"Das Wahlsystem." *Landeszentrale für politische Bildung Baden-Württemberg.* Web. 28 Jan. 2017.

seats in the "Bundestag"[71]. In order to limit the number of parties in the "Bundestag", only parties who receive at least five percent of all votes get seats in the "Bundestag". This law is called "Fünf-Prozent-Hürde" and it was made to prevent a parliament with seventeen parties as it had been the case during the Weimar Republic[72]. As mentioned before, the "Bundestag" has 598 delegates. Half of them are elected by the first vote and the remainder is determined by the second vote of each voter[73]. The majority of the "Landtagswahlen" are also based on personal proportional representation. Only the state of Saarland uses a proportional representation[74]. In almost all federal states, the elections of the governments of the communes are based on the proportional representation. Only North Rhine-Westphalia uses the personal proportional representation for local elections[75].

2.2.2 The party system of Germany

In the "Bundesrepublik Deutschland", there are a lot of political parties to choose from, which results in a true multiple party system[76]. The dominant party in Germany is the "Christlich Demokratische Union Deutschland" (CDU) which received 41.5 percent of the vote during the most recent parliamentary election for the "Bundestag" in 2013[77]. It is the party which gets the most votes in the rural areas[78]. The "Sozialdemokratische Partei Deutschland" (SPD) which got 25.7 percent at the last parliamentary election for the "Bundestag" in 2013[79] is the party which gets the most votes in the German cities[80]. Other parties that are represented in the "Bundestag" are "Die Grünen", which was founded by the anti-nuclear movement in the 70s and 80s[81], the "Freie Demokratische Partei", "Die Linke" and the "Alternative für Deutschland"[82].

[71]Korte, Karl-Rudolf. *Wahlen in Deutschland*.
[72]"Die Fünf-Prozent-Hürde- Infos und Erklärungen." *Welt*. Web. 28 Jan. 2017.
[73]"Wahl der Abgeordneten und Mandatsverteilung." *Deutscher Bundestag*. Web. 28 Jan. 2017.
[74]Zicht, Wilko. "Landtagswahlrecht." *Wahlrecht*. Web. 27 Jan. 2017.
[75]Zicht, Wilko. "Komunalwahlrecht." *Wahlrecht*. Web. 28 Jan. 2017.
[76]Egle, Gert. "Parteiensystem in Der Bundesrepublik Deutschland Überblick." *Teachsam*. Web. 7 Feb. 2017.
[77]Zicht, Wilko. "Ergebnisse Der Bundestagswahlen." *Wahlrecht*. Web. 7 Feb. 2017.
[78]Ellermann, Viktoria, and Manuel Werder. "Konfliktlinien im deutschen Parteiensystem." *Abi-Box Politik-Wirtschaft: Demokratie und Sozialer Rechtsstaat*. 60.
[79]Zicht, Wilko. "Ergebnisse Der Bundestagswahlen." *Wahlrecht*. Web. 7 Feb. 2017.
[80]Ellermann, Viktoria, and Manuel Werder. "Konfliktlinien im deutschen Parteiensystem." *Abi-Box Politik-Wirtschaft: Demokratie und Sozialer Rechtsstaat*. 60.
[81]Hofmann, Rebecca. "Entstehung Der Grünen." *Planet Wissen*. Web. 7 Feb. 2017.
[82]Egle, Gert. "Parteiensystem in Der Bundesrepublik Deutschland Überblick." *Teachsam*. Web. 7 Feb. 2017.

3 The governmental system of the United States of America

3.1 The historical development of the governmental system of the United States of America

Towards the end of the 15th century, European countries and later especially the United Kingdom established colonies in North America[83].

In the second half of the 18th century, the United Kingdom imposed more and more taxes and restrictions on its North American colonies because of the bad economic situation at home. In response to the increasing pressure from King George III, representatives of 12 of the 13 all British colonies in North America met at the first Continental Congress in 1774[84]. Many people that would later play an important role in America´s future attended. Among them were George Washington (first president of USA in future)[85] and John Adams (second president of USA in future)[86]. At the first Continental Congress, the participants claimed that the British government dismiss the tea tax. This resulted in an overreaction by the British government which feared the start of a rebellion. This conflict subsequently led to the American Revolutionary War from 1775 until 1783[87]. The first Continental army, which was led by George Washington, fought against the British army[88]. At the Second Continental Congress in July 1776, Thomas Jefferson, who would later become the third president of the USA, drafted the Declaration of Independence[89]. The thirteen colonies, which had mostly been independent of each other until then, became the first thirteen American states[90]. Each state had one vote in Congress, which is considered the first national political institution with still very limited political power at the time[91].

In 1778, the United States Constitution was written by 55 members of Congress under the leadership of George Washington. It has been the political foundation of the United States ever since[92]. For instance, the electoral system was outlined in this original Constitution. It also included a clause that denied African-Americans the right to vote.

---

[83]"Die Englischen Kolonien in Amerika." *Lernhelfer.* Web. 14 Feb. 2017.
[84]"Amerikanischer Unabhängigkeitskrieg." *Geschichte Kompakt.* Web. 14 Feb. 2017.
[85]Freidel, Frank, and Hugh Sidey. "George Washington." *White House.* Web. 10 Feb. 2017.
[86]Freidel, Frank, and Hugh Sidey. "John Adams." *White House.* Web. 10 Feb. 2017.
[87]"Amerikanischer Unabhängigkeitskrieg." *Geschichte Kompakt.* Web. 14 Feb. 2017.
[88]"George Washington." *Lernhelfer.* Web. 14 Feb. 2017.
[89]Oldopp, Birgit. *Das politische System der USA, Eine Einführung.* 15.
[90]ibid. 16.
[91]"1. Kongress Der Vereinigten Staaten." *Wikipedia.* Web. 14 Feb. 2017.
[92]Bos, Ellen. "Die Geschichte Der Modernen Verfassungen Im Überblick." Verfassungsgebung Und Systemwechsel: Die Institutionalisierung Von Demokratie Im Postsozialistischen Osteuropa. Web. 14 Feb. 2017.

Moreover, today's division of power and institutions of governance also go back to this Constitution of 1778[93].

Because of the fact that a lot of immigrants came to the USA from Europe and that the USA territory was expanded during the 19th century, new federal states like California (1850) and Missouri (1821) were admitted to the union[94]. In the middle of the 19th century, conflicts about slavery arose between the northern states and the southern states. The northern states, which were much more industrialized than the southern, rejected slavery, but the southern states needed slaves, because they provided cheap labour on cotton plantations, which were the economic mainstay of the southern states[95]. Leaving the USA, the southern states founded the Confederate States of America (CSA)[96] and attacked Union soldiers at Fort Sumter, South Carolina on April 12, 1861. This marked the start of the American Civil War that lasted until 1865[97]. Three days after the capitulation of the CSA and the end of the Civil War, Abraham Lincoln, who had been President of the USA since 1860[98], was assassinated by a fanatic Southerner[99].

After the Civil War, the southern states re-joined the USA and slavery was forbidden by the thirteenth amendment to the Constitution[100]. However, the discrimination against African-Americans did not stop. In 1896, the US Supreme Court upheld segregation between white and black people in public places[101]. This meant, for example, that African-Americans had seats separate from white people in theatres or on public transport: African-Americans had to sit in the back of the bus[102].

At the beginning of the First Wold War, the USA did not fight in Europe. But in 1917, when German submarines sank three American ships, the USA declared war on Germany and helped win it[103].

Before the United States fought in the Second World War from 1941 to 1945 and won together with other countries like the United Kingdom and France[104], there had been a

---

[93]"Verfassungen Der Vereinigten Staaten Von Amerika." Verfassungen.net. Web. 14 Feb. 2017.
[94]"Geschichte Der Vereinigten Staaten." Wikipedia. Web. 14 Feb. 2017.
[95]Amerikanische Geschichte Erklärt: Verfassung & Bürgerkrieg (2/2). Perf. MrWissen2go. Youtube. Web. 14 Feb. 2017.
[96]"Konföderierte Staaten Von Amerika." Lexas. Web. 14 Feb. 2017.
[97]"Der Amerikanische Bürgerkrieg (Sezessionskrieg) 1861-1865." Landesbildungsserver Baden-Württemberg. Web. 14 Feb. 2017.
[98]Krauel, Torsten. "Wo Geld Nach Freiheit Duftet." Welt Am Sonntag. 2-3.
[99]Schweitzer, Eva. ""Dann Werden Sie Es Mit Der Kugel Tun"." Spiegel Online. Web. 14 Feb. 2017.
[100]Langels, Otto. "Für Ein Amerika Ohne Sklaverei." Deutschlandfunk. Web. 14 Feb. 2017.
[101]"Rassentrennung Für Legal Erklärt." Welt. Web. 14 Feb. 2017.
[102]Schmid, Michael. "Vor 50 Jahren: Busboykott in Montgomery." *Lebenshaus Schwäbisch Alb*. Web. 14 Feb. 2017.
[103]Spörl, Gerhard. "Feldzug Der Friedliebenden." *Spiegel Online*. Web. 14 Feb. 2017.
[104]"US-Geschichte Der Zweite Weltkrieg." *About the USA*. Web. 14 Feb. 2017.

world economic crisis in 1929, which lasted until the mid-1930s[105]. After the Second World War, the nuclear arms race started between the USA and the Soviet Union and the two countries entered the period of the Cold War that did not end until the 1990s[106].

American rights and laws also changed during this time. According to the nineteenth article of the constitution, women received the right to vote on the 28th of August in 1920[107], while African-Americans did not receive the unconditional right to vote until the sixth of August, 1965. This was a giant leap for equality in the USA[108].

While the segregation between the white and black people in the USA officially ended in 1964, the election of the first African-American president, Barack Obama, in 2009[109] marked another major milestone in overcoming the effects of segregation.

[105]"Die Weltwirtschaftskrise 1929-1932." *Geschichte-Wissen*. Web. 14 Feb. 2017.
[106]Stöver, Bernd. "Der Kalte Krieg Und Das Wettrüsten." *Bundeszentrale Für Politische Bildung*. Web. 14 Feb. 2017.
[107]"Wahlrecht Für Frauen." *Berliner Zeitung*. Web. 14 Feb. 2017.
[108]"Wahlrecht Für Afro-Amerikaner." *Was Ist Was*. Web. 14 Feb. 2017.
[109]"Barack Obama Wird Neuer Präsident Der USA." *Auswärtiges Amt*. Web. 14 Feb. 2017.

3.2 The political system of the United States of America

Every political process in the USA is based on the Constitution. The governmental system of the USA is a presidential democracy[110] with three branches of power[111]: The legislative, the executive and the judicial branch[112]. The Congress, which represents the legislative branch, consists of the Senate and the House of Representatives[113]. The President of the USA and his cabinet form the executive branch[114], and the Supreme Court is the highest court of the judicial branch[115]. The division of power is called "checks and balances". This means that the political institutions monitor each other[116] to prevent any political institution from becoming too powerful[117].

The Senate is made up of two delegates from each state.[118] There have been a total of one hundred senators[119] since 1959[120]. The Vice President of the United States, Mike Pence, serves as the president of the Senate[121] and casts the deciding vote in case of a tie[122]. The most important task of the Senate is the passing of legislation together with the House of Representatives except for tax laws, which are exclusively made by the House of Representatives. Giving advice to the President in matters of nominations for ambassadors or judges to the Supreme Court is an important task of the Senate as well[123]. The Senate also has to ratify international contracts the USA enters into[124].

The second institution of Congress is the House of Representatives with 435 lawmakers. How many members of the House of Representatives come from each state depends on a state's population[125]. For instance, there are fifty-three delegates from California and only one from South Dakota[126]. Like the Senate, the House of Representatives meets in

---

[110]Pawlak, Britta. "USA-Vereinigte Staaten Von Amerika." *Helles Köpfchen.de*. Web. 4 Feb. 2017.
[111]Hoffmann, Lars. "Politisches System Der USA." *Americanet*. Web. 4 Feb. 2017.
[112]"Gewaltenteilung - Politisches System Der USA." *Magazin USA.com*. Web. 4 Feb. 2017.
[113]Hoffmann, Lars. "Legislative." *Americanet*. Web. 4 Feb. 2017.
[114]Hoffmann, Lars. "Exekutive." *Americanet*. Web. 4 Feb. 2017.
[115]Hoffmann, Lars. "Judikative." *Americanet*. Web. 4 Feb. 2017.
[116]Braml, Josef. "Konkurrenz Und Kontrolle Der Machthaber: Checks and Balances." *Bundeszentrale Für Politische Bildung*. Web. 5 Feb. 2017.
[117]Hoffmann, Lars. "Checks and Balances." *Americanet*. Web. 5 Feb. 2017.
[118]"United States Senate." *United States Senate*. Web. 4 Feb. 2017.
[119] "Senat Der Vereinigten Staaten." *Wikipedia*. Web. 4 Feb. 2017.
[120]Gellner, Winand, and Martin Kleiber. "Der Senat." *Das Regierungssystem Der USA, Eine Einführung*. 39.
[121] "Gewaltenteilung - Politisches System Der USA." *Magazin USA.com*. Web. 4 Feb. 2017.
[122]Gersch, Clemens. "Hintergrund: Die Macht des amerikanischen Präsidenten." *Planet Schule*. Web. 4 Feb. 2017.
[123]Hoffmann, Lars. "Legislative." *Americanet*. Web. 4 Feb. 2017.
[124]ibid
[125]"Wahlen, Hintergrund: Senat Und Repräsentantenhaus Im US-Kongress." *Focus Online*. Web. 4 Feb. 2017.
[126]"Repräsentantenhaus Der Vereinigten Staaten." *Wikipedia*. Web. 4 Feb. 2017.

the Capitol Building in Washington D.C[127]. The members of the House of Representatives are able to initiate impeachment proceeding than can result in the removal of the President of the USA from office[128]. So far, only three presidents have been subject to impeachment proceedings in the history of the United States, and none of them resulted in the removal of the President from office – President Nixon resigned before he could be impeached[129]. So another one of the important tasks of the Senate and the House of Representatives is the supervision of the President[130].

Donald Trump has been the President of the USA since the 20th of January in 2017,[131] and he lives and works in the White House in Washington D.C.[132]. The President is the centre of the political power in the governmental system of the USA[133]. He simultaneously serves as the head of state, the head of government[134] and the commander in chief of the military forces[135]. The most important task of the President is implementation of the decisions made in Congress. He is able to propose laws as well as veto any laws coming out of Congress[136]. He also nominates ambassadors and judges to the Supreme Court as mentioned before[137].

The President is supported by his ministers and Presidential Commissions which are both considered part of the executive, too[138]. Another executive institution is the Executive Office of the President, which consists of the White House Office, the Office of Management and Budget and the National Security Council and is responsible for the federal budget and advising the President[139].

The Supreme Court is the only court explicitly mentioned in the Constitution of the United States, but the Constitution allows for the establishment of lower courts on an as needed

---

[127]"Kongress - Fragmentierte Legislative." *Bundeszentrale Für Politische Bildung*. Web. 4 Feb. 2017.
[128]Gellner, Winand, and Martin Kleiber. "Der Senat." *Das Regierungssystem Der USA, Eine Einführung*. 40.
[129]Strutynski, Peter. "Warum Es Noch Kein Impeachment-Verfahren gegen US-Präsident George W. Bush Gibt." *AG Friedensforschung*. Web. 4 Feb. 2017.
[130]"Kongress - Fragmentierte Legislative." *Bundeszentrale Für Politische Bildung*. Web. 4 Feb. 2017.
[131]"Donald Trump." *Zeit Online*. Web. 4 Feb. 2017.
[132]"Weißes Haus in Washington." *Washington-reise.de*. Web. 5 Feb. 2017.
[133]Gersch, Clemens. "Hintergrund: Die Macht des amerikanischen Präsidenten." *Planet Schule*. Web. 4 Feb. 2017.
[134]Hoffmann, Lars. "Exekutive." *Americanet*. Web. 4 Feb. 2017.
[135]Gersch, Clemens. "Hintergrund: Die Macht des amerikanischen Präsidenten." *Planet Schule*. Web. 4 Feb. 2017.
[136]"Gewaltenteilung - Politisches System Der USA." *Magazin USA.com*. Web. 4 Feb.
[137]Hoffmann, Lars. "Legislative." *Americanet*. Web. 4 Feb. 2017.
[138]Hoffmann, Lars. "Exekutive." *Americanet*. Web. 4 Feb. 2017.
[139]"Politisches System Der Vereinigten Staaten." *Wikipedia*. Web. 5 Feb. 2017.

basis[140]. Currently, there are nine judges on the Supreme Court. Most of the time, the Supreme Court is utilized as a court of appeals. If there is a claimant who thinks a lower court did not treat him right, the Supreme Court can take on the case[141]. The judges of the Supreme Court also decide about lawsuits that involve a state[142].

In addition to the governmental system on the national level, each state has its own constitution and government. The state governments are also divided into three different branches[143]. Everywhere except for Nebraska the legislative branch is subdivided into two parliaments[144]. The governor of a state is directly elected by the citizens of the state and represents the highest institution of the executive branch[145]. It is remarkable that other political functionaries are also directly elected by the citizens[146].

<u>3.2.1 The electoral system of the United States of America</u>

Since 1789, there have been fifty-eight presidential elections in the United States of America[147]. Presidential elections take place every four years. Each person who is at least eighteen years old and is a citizen of the USA has the right to vote for the President[148]. If a person has the passport of the USA, is at least 35 years old and has lived in the USA for the last fourteen years, the person can be a presidential candidate. A president is limited to serve a maximum of two terms[149]. The election of the US President is an indirect election where registered voters of each state elect electors, which 41 days later then cast direct votes for President and Vice president of the United States[150]. In all states except for Nebraska and Maine the "Winner-takes-all"-principle applies, which means that all electors of that state vote for the presidential candidate from the party that received the most votes in their state. Therefore, it is possible that the candidate who receives the most votes does not win the election[151]. As the following graphics show,

---

[140]"Oberster Gerichtshof Der Vereinigten Staaten." *Wikipedia*. Web. 5 Feb. 2017.
[141]Hoffmann, Lars. "Judikative." *Americanet*. Web. 4 Feb. 2017.
[142]"Oberster Gerichtshof Der Vereinigten Staaten." *Wissen.de*. Web. 5 Feb. 2017.
[143]Gellner, Winand, and Martin Kleiber. "Vertikale Gewaltenteilung-Föderalismus in Deutschland." *Das Regierungssystem der USA, Eine Einführung*. 128.
[144]Prof. Dr. Lösche, Peter. "US-Föderalismus." *Bundeszentrale Für Politische Bildung*. Web. 5 Feb. 2017.
[145]Gellner, Winand, and Martin Kleiber. "Vertikale Gewaltenteilung-Föderalismus in Deutschland." *Das Regierungssystem der USA, Eine Einführung*. 128.
[146]Prof. Dr. Lösche, Peter. "US-Föderalismus." *Bundeszentrale Für Politische Bildung*. Web. 5 Feb. 2017.
[147]"US-Wahlen 2016." Focus Online. Web. 1 Feb. 2017.
[148]Oelker, Laura, and Sybille Klormann. "Wie wird der US-Präsident gewählt?" Zeit Online. Web. 1 Feb. 2017.
[149]Oldopp, Birgit. Das politische System der USA, Eine Einführung. 159.
[150]Munk, Stephanie. "US-Wahl 2016: Die wichtigsten Fragen und Antworten." Merkur. Web. 1 Feb. 2017.
[151]Oelker, Laura, and Sybille Klormann. "Wie wird der US-Präsident gewählt?" Zeit Online. Web. 1 Feb. 2017.

Hillary Clinton had more votes in the last election. But finally, Donald Trump won the election, because he got the majority of the votes of electoral delegates in more states.

On top of this, the number of electors of a state is equal to the number of delegates in Congress (House of Representatives and Senate) of that state. For instance, California has the most electors (fifty-five) and Alaska, Vermont, South Dakota, North Dakota, Montana, Delaware, Wyoming and Washington D.C. have the fewest number of electors (three each)[152]. Two months after the electors have voted, the term of office of the new President starts[153].

In addition to the presidential elections, there are elections to the House of Representatives and the Senate in the United States of America.

The citizens of each of the 435 election districts elect one delegate of the House of Representatives every two years in a general, equal, free and secret election[154]. Any person who is at least eighteen years old and a citizen of the USA has the right to vote for delegates of the House of Representatives as well as to the Senate[155].

The election of the Senate takes place every two years,[156] but only one third of the senators are elected every two years, so the delegates of the Senate have the opportunity to be in office for six years[157].

[152]"Electoral College." *Wikipedia*. Web. 1 Feb. 2017.
[153]"Das sollten sie jetzt zur Wahl von Donald Trump wissen." *Welt*. Web. 1 Feb. 2017.
[154]"Repräsentantenhaus Der Vereinigten Staaten." *Wikipedia*. Web. 4 Feb. 2017.
[155]Fehndrich, Martin. "US-Repräsentantenhaus." *Wahlrecht*. Web. 13 Feb. 2017.
[156]Fehndrich, Martin. "US-Senat." *Wahlrecht*. Web. 12 Feb. 2017.
[157]Stevenson, Scot. "Amerikaner Wählen Alle Zwei Jahre." *N-TV*. Web. 3 Feb. 2017.

3.2.2 The party system of the United States of America

Because of the fact that there are only two parties in the United States who receive enough votes to establish a government, it is a two-party system[158]. The Democratic Party and the Republican Party have been in power for 150 years. The Democrats, which were founded in 1828,[159] are a liberal party that represents the working class and pick up topics like civil liberties[160]. The Republicans, which were founded in 1854,[161] are a conservative party and campaign for topics like tax reduction, or a strong army[162]. Despite the dominance of these two parties, there are some other parties like the Green Party, the Constitution Party, and the Libertarian Party[163].

---

[158]Gellner, Winand, and Martin Kleiber. "Parteien und Gewaltenteilung." *Das Regierungssystem der USA, Eine Einführung.* 142.
[159]"Washington (dpa) - In Den USA Gibt Es Im Wesentlichen Zwei Große Konkurrierende Parteien:." *Web.de.* Web. 7 Feb. 2017.
[160]Radler, Christian. "Land Der Zwei-Parteien Herrschaft." *Tagesschau.de.* Web. 7 Feb. 2017.
[161]"Washington (dpa) - In Den USA Gibt Es Im Wesentlichen Zwei Große Konkurrierende Parteien:." *Web.de.* Web. 7 Feb. 2017.
[162]Radler, Christian. "Land Der Zwei-Parteien Herrschaft." *Tagesschau.de.* Web. 7 Feb. 2017.
[163]"Parteien in den USA." *Landeszentrale Für Politische Bildung Baden-Württemberg.* Web. 7 Feb. 2017.

4 Comparison: Similarities and Differences

After describing the individual governmental systems of Germany and the United States of America in the previous section, the following section will examine the differences between and similarities of the German and the American governmental system. The biggest difference between the two systems is the fact, that the German system is organized as a parliamentary democracy,[164] while the American system is organized as a presidential democracy[165]. Parliamentary democracy means that the citizens elect a parliament which then forms the government[166] and therefore gives the citizens a lot of influence on the politics in their country. A presidential democracy means that the president is directly or indirectly elected by the citizens, serves as the head of government and the head of state[167] and is the political centre of the executive branch[168].

The German legislative branch on the national level is divided into the "Bundestag" and the "Bundesrat"[169]. Moreover, the "Bundestag" is elected by the citizens on the national level[170], but the "Bundesrat" consists of members of the state governments[171]. The American legislative branch is divided in two institutions as well. It consists of the Senate and the House of Representatives and both institutions are directly elected by the citizens on a national level[172]. The difference between the German parliament and the US Congress is that the German executive branch is made up of members of the German parliament where the US executive branch is independent from the US Congress.

Furthermore, in the USA there are only two big parties, the "Republican Party" and the "Democratic Party"[173]. In Germany there are many more important parties. Some examples are "Bündnis 90/Die Grünen", "CDU", "SPD", "Die Linke" and a relatively new party "Die Alternative für Deutschland"[174].

Germany is divided into sixteen federal states. They are called "Bundesländer" and all of them have their own government[175], which is, for example, responsible for the police and

---

[164]"Parlamentarische Demokratie." *Bundeszentrale Für Politische Bildung*. Web. 12 Feb. 2017.
[165]Lösche, Peter. "Merkmale Der US-Präsidialdemokratie." *Wissen.de*. Web. 12 Feb. 2017.
[166]"Parlamentarische Demokratie." *Bundeszentrale Für Politische Bildung*. Web. 12 Feb. 2017.
[167]Lösche, Peter. "Merkmale Der US-Präsidialdemokratie." *Wissen.de*. Web. 12 Feb. 2017.
[168]Gersch, Clemens. "Hintergrund: Die Macht des amerikanischen Präsidenten." *Planet Schule*. Web. 12 Feb. 2017.
[169]"Gewaltenteilung." *Deutsch-werden.de*. Web. 12 Feb. 2017.
[170]Ellermann, Viktoria, and Manuel Werder. "Der Deutsche Bundestag." *Abi-Box Politik-Wirtschaft: Demokratie und Sozialer Rechtsstaat*. 80.
[171]ibid. 84.
[172]Hoffmann, Lars. "Legislative." *Americanet*. Web. 4 Feb. 2017.
[173]Radler, Christian. "Land Der Zwei-Parteien Herrschaft." *Tagesschau.de*. Web. 7 Feb. 2017.
[174]Egle, Gert. "Parteiensystem in Der Bundesrepublik Deutschland Überblick." *Teachsam*. Web. 7 Feb. 2017.
[175]"Die Bundesländer Deutschlands." *Allgemeinwissen.com*. Web. 29 Jan. 2017.

public education. In the USA, there are 50 federal states with individual state governments as well[176].

While the "Bundeskanzler" is elected by the "Bundestag"[177], the President of the USA is indirectly elected by the citizens[178]. Moreover, the members of the cabinet of Germany also are delegates of the "Bundestag", while the members of the American cabinet are not members of Congress[179]. Aside from that, the executive branch in Germany is divided into the "Bundeskanzler", who is the head of government and the "Bundespräsident", who is the head of state[180]. As mentioned before, the American executive is not divided, because the president is the head of state and the head of government simultaneously[181].

There are also some differences between the election systems. For instance, the American people who have the right to vote have to register to vote as there is no compulsory registration with the local communes in the US[182], while the German citizens get a polling card before the election due to being registered in their municipality[183]. Moreover, the election of the "Bundestag" is based on personal proportional representation[184] and the election system of the USA is based on the majority voting system[185]. The election turnout in Germany is higher than the turnout in the USA. For instance, there was an election turnout of 71.5 percent at the last election of the Bundestag[186], while the turnout of the last presidential election was only 58.9 percent[187].

While the judges of the Supreme Court are nominated by the President and hold their position for life[188], the judges of the "Bundesgerichtshof" are elected every twelve years[189].

[176]"Bundesstaaten Der USA – 50 Einzelne Gliedstaaten." *USA Tipps*. Web. 13 Feb. 2017.
[177]Ellermann, Viktoria, and Manuel Werder. "Der Deutsche Bundestag." *Abi-Box Politik-Wirtschaft: Demokratie und Sozialer Rechtsstaat*. 80.
[178]"US-Wahlen 2016." *Focus Online*. Web. 1 Feb. 2017.
[179]"Wahlen, Hintergrund: Senat Und Repräsentantenhaus Im US-Kongress." *Focus Online*. Web. 4 Feb. 2017.
[180]"Kanzleramt." *Die Bundeskanzlerin*. Web. 13 Feb. 2017.
[181]Gersch, Clemens. "Hintergrund: Die Macht des amerikanischen Präsidenten." *Planet Schule*. Web. 4 Feb. 2017.
[182]Oelker, Laura, and Sybille Klormann. "Wie wird der US-Präsident gewählt?" *Zeit Online*. Web. 1 Feb. 2017.
[183]Schneider, Gerd, and Christiane Toyka-Seid. "Wahlbenachrichtigung." *Bundeszentrale Für Politische Bildung*. Web. 14 Feb. 2017.
[184]Korte, Karl-Rudolf. "Das Personalisierte Verhältniswahlrecht." *Bundeszentrale Für Politische Bildung*. Web. 14 Feb. 2017.
[185]"Mehrheitswahlrecht: Das "Winner-takes-all"-Prinzip." *Zeit Online*. Web. 14 Feb. 2017.
[186]"Wahlbeteiligung Bei Bundestagswahlen." *Bundestagswahl 2017*. Web. 14 Feb. 2017.
[187]"Wie Hoch War Die Wahlbeteiligung Bei Den US-Wahlen 2016?" *Landeszentrale Für Politische Bildung Baden-Württemberg*. Web. 14 Feb. 2017.
[188]"Trump Will Obersten Richter Am Dienstag Benennen." *Zeit Online*. Web. 14 Feb. 2017.
[189]"Die Richterinnen Und Richter Des Bundesverfassungsgerichts." *Bundesverfassungsgericht*. Web. 14 Feb. 2017.

Another difference is that the American system is more than 230 years old[190] while the German one has only about 65 years of experience[191].

Summarising the similarities and differences it can be concluded that the German governmental system and the one of the USA are similarly organized, but there are some important differences like the positions of the "Bundeskanzler" of Germany and the President of the United States.

---

[190]Oldopp, Birgit. *Das politische System der USA, Eine Einführung.* 16.
[191]Küsters, Hanns Jürgen. "Gründung Der Bundesrepublik Deutschland 1949." *Konrad Adenauer.* Web. 10 Feb. 2017.

5 Conclusion

Considering the similarities and differences, the two systems are quite similar to each other in some parts. Especially, the legislative and the judicial branches have many things in common. However, the executive branches of power are significantly different in the two systems. For example, the President of the USA is more powerful than the "Bundeskanzlerin" because he is the head of state and the head of government[192] while the "Bundeskanzlerin" is only the head of government[193].

As a conclusion of the comparison, both governmental systems have their advantages and disadvantages. Because of that it is not possible to say which is the better one. But if each country took some ideas of the other, it could be useful for their development in future. For instance, the USA could modernize its 200-year-old presidential election system by establishing a system like Germany's which is based on personal proportional representation[194]. And Germany could concentrate a little bit more on representative tasks of high-ranking German politicians to create a better symbolic status like the U.S. President is doing all the time.

All in all, it will be really interesting to observe which system exists longer and is better positioned to overcome the problems of the world in future.

6 Bibliography

"1. Kongress Der Vereinigten Staaten." *Wikipedia*. N.p., n.d. Web. 14 Feb. 2017. <https://de.wikipedia.org/wiki/1._Kongress_der_Vereinigten_Staaten>.

Amerikanische Geschichte Erklärt: Verfassung & Bürgerkrieg (2/2). Perf. MrWissen2go. *Youtube*. N.p. 5.11-6.04, 23 Oct. 2013. Web. 14 Feb. 2017. <https://www.youtube.com/watch?v=khcRBxnnou4>.

"Amerikanischer Unabhängigkeitskrieg." *Geschichte Kompakt*. N.p., n.d. Web. 14 Feb. 2017. <http://www.geschichte-abitur.de/ancien-regime/unabhangigkeitskrieg>.

---

[192]Lösche, Peter. "Merkmale Der US-Präsidialdemokratie." *Wissen.de*. Web. 12 Feb. 2017.
[193]"Kanzleramt." *Die Bundeskanzlerin*. Web. 13 Feb. 2017.
[194]Korte, Karl-Rudolf. "Das Personalisierte Verhältniswahlrecht." *Bundeszentrale Für Politische Bildung*. Web. 14 Feb. 2017.

"Barack Obama Wird Neuer Präsident Der USA." *Auswärtiges Amt.* N.p., 07 Nov. 2008.
Web. 14 Feb. 2017.
<http://www.kinder.diplo.de/Vertretung/kinder/de/__pr/Amerika/081107-
Obama.html?archive=2403278>.

"Bildungsexpansion Und Schulreform in Der Bundesrepublik." *Chroniknet.* N.p., n.d. Web.
14 Feb. 2017. <https://chroniknet.de/extra/zeitgeschichte/1970-bildungsexpansion-und-
schulreform-in-der-bundesrepublik/>.

Bognanni, Massimo. "Politisches System der Bundesrepublik Deutschland." *Zeit Online.*
N.p., 10 Sept. 2010. Web. 31 Jan. 2017. <http://blog.zeit.de/schueler/2010/09/10/thema-
politisches-system-der-bundesrepublik-deutschland/>.

Bos, Ellen. "Die Geschichte Der Modernen Verfassungen Im Überblick."
*Verfassungsgebung Und Systemwechsel: Die Institutionalisierung Von Demokratie Im
Postsozialistischen Osteuropa.* Wiesbaden: VS Verlag Für Sozialwissenschaften, 2004.
84. *Google Books.* Web. 14 Feb. 2017.
<https://books.google.de/books?id=9_0mBgAAQBAJ&pg=PA83&lpg=PA83&dq=verfassu
ngsgebung+usa&source=bl&ots=So_8u28Iqb&sig=1dP9HbuuDcSm4EZA_w0THjMruW8
&hl=de&sa=X&ved=0ahUKEwikl-
q4s4_SAhXmO5oKHdrABOUQ6AEIMzAD#v=onepage&q=verfassungsgebung%20usa&f
=false>.

Braml, Josef. "Konkurrenz Und Kontrolle Der Machthaber: Checks and Balances."
Bundeszentrale Für Politische Bildung. N.p., 12 June 2014. Web. 5 Feb. 2017.
<https://www.bpb.de/izpb/186246/konkurrenz-und-kontrolle-der-machthaber-checks-and-
balances>.

"Bundespräsidentin Malu Dreyer." *Bundesrat.* N.p., n.d. Web. 31 Jan. 2017.
<http://www.bundesrat.de/DE/bundesrat/praesidium/praesident/praesident-node.html>.

"Bundesstaaten Der USA – 50 Einzelne Gliedstaaten." *USA Tipps.* N.p., n.d. Web. 13
Feb. 2017. <http://www.usatipps.de/bundesstaaten/>.

"Bundestagswahl 2017." *Der Bundeswahlleiter.* N.p., n.d. Web. 27 Jan.
2017.<https://www.bundeswahlleiter.de/bundestagswahlen/2017.html>.

"Bundestagswahlen 2013." *Landeszentrale für politische Bildung Baden-Württenberg.* N.p., n.d. Web. 27 Jan. 2017. <http://www.bundestagswahl-bw.de/uebersicht_bundestagswahl.html>.

Carrasco, Ines. "Studentenbewegung." *Planet Wissen.* N.p., 20 Aug. 2014. Web. 10 Feb. 2017. <http://www.planet-wissen.de/geschichte/deutsche_geschichte/studentenbewegung/>.

"Das sollten sie jetzt zur Wahl von Donald Trump wissen." *Welt.* N.p., 10 Nov. 2016. Web. 1 Feb. 2017. <https://www.welt.de/politik/ausland/article159394281/Das-sollten-Sie-jetzt-zur-Wahl-von-Donald-Trump-wissen.html>.

"Das Wahlsystem." *Landeszentrale für politische Bildung Baden-Württemberg.* N.p., n.d. Web. 28 Jan. 2017. <http://www.bundestagswahl-bw.de/wahlsystem1.html>.

"Demonstrationen in Der Ganzen DDR." *Jugendopposition.* Bundeszentrale Für Politische Bildung Und Robert-Havemann-Gesellschaft E.V, Sept. 2008. Web. 7 Feb. 2017. <http://www.jugendopposition.de/index.php?id=212>.

"Der Amerikanische Bürgerkrieg (Sezessionskrieg) 1861-1865." *Landesbildungsserver Baden-Württemberg.* N.p., n.d. Web. 14 Feb. 2017. <http://www.schule-bw.de/unterricht/faecher/geschichte/unterricht/unterrichtsekl/19jahrhundert/usasek1/seze ssionskrieg/>.

"Die aktuellen Ministerpräsidenten der deutschen Bundesländer." *Wissen.de.* N.p., n.d. Web. 29 Jan. 2017.< http://www.wissen.de/lexikon/die-aktuellen-ministerpraesidenten-der-deutschen-bundeslaender>.

"Die bisherigen Wahlperioden des Bundestages." *Kürschners Politikkontakte.* N.p., n.d. Web. 27 Jan. 2017. <https://www.ndv.info/2013/12/11/die-bisherigen-wahlperioden-des-bundestages/>.

"Die Bundesländer Deutschlands." *Allgemeinwissen.com.* N.p., 12 May 2016. Web. 29 Jan. 2017.< http://allgemeinwissen.com/2016/05/12/die-bundeslaender-deutschlands/>.

"Die Bundespräsidentenwahl 2017." *Landeszentrale für politische Bildung Baden-Württemberg*. N.p., n.d. Web. 31 Jan. 2017. <https://www.lpb-bw.de/bundespraesidentenwahl_2017.html>.

"Die Englischen Kolonien in Amerika." *Lernhelfer*. N.p., 2010. Web. 14 Feb. 2017. <https://www.lernhelfer.de/schuelerlexikon/geschichte/artikel/die-englischen-kolonien-amerika>.

"Die Fünf-Prozent-Hürde- Infos und Erklärungen." *Welt*. N.p., 05 June 2013. Web. 28 Jan. 2017. <https://www.welt.de/politik/wahl/bundestagswahl/article115983477/Die-Fuenf-Prozent-Huerde-Infos-Erklaerungen.html>.

"Die Gesetzgebung des Bundes." *Deutscher Bundestag*. N.p., n.d. Web. 31 Jan. 2017. <https://www.bundestag.de/parlament/aufgaben/rechtsgrundlagen/grundgesetz/gg_07/24 5138>.

"Die Richterinnen Und Richter Des Bundesverfassungsgerichts." *Bundesverfassungsgericht*. N.p., n.d. Web. 14 Feb. 2017. <http://www.bundesverfassungsgericht.de/DE/Richter/richter_node.html>.

"Die Weltwirtschaftskrise 1929-1932." *Geschichte-Wissen*. N.p., 27 Oct. 2009. Web. 14 Feb. 2017. <http://geschichte-wissen.de/blog/die-weltwirtschaftskrise-1929-1932/>.

"Die Ziele Der Alliierten 1945-1949." *Konrad Adenauer Stiftung*. N.p., n.d. Web. 10 Feb. 2017. <http://www.kas.de/wf/de/71.6595/>.

"Donald Trump." *Zeit Online*. N.p., n.d. Web. 4 Feb. 2017. <http://www.zeit.de/thema/donald-trump>.

Egle, Gert. "Parteiensystem in Der Bundesrepublik Deutschland Überblick." *Teachsam*. N.p., 06 Aug. 2016. Web. 7 Feb. 2017. <http://www.teachsam.de/politik/brd_pols/parteien/brd_parteien_5_1.htm>.

"Electoral College." *Wikipedia*. N.p., n.d. Web. 1 Feb. 2017. <https://de.wikipedia.org/wiki/Electoral_College>.

Ellermann, Viktoria, and Manuel Werder. *Abi-Box Politik-Wirtschaft: Demokratie und Sozialer Rechtsstaat.* Hannover: Brinkmann Meyerhöfer GmbH & KG, 2016. 60-87. Print.

"Ergebnis Der US-Wahl Im Jahr 2016 Nach Anteil Der Wählerstimmen." *Statista.* N.p., 08 Nov. 2016. Web. 19 Feb. 2017. <https://de.statista.com/statistik/daten/studie/630975/umfrage/endergebnis-der-us-praesidentschaftswahl-2016-nach-anteil-der-waehlerstimmen/>.

"Ergebnis Der US-Wahl Im Jahr 2016 Nach Anzahl Der Gewonnenen Wahlmänner." *Statista.* N.p., 08 Nov. 2016. Web. 19 Feb. 2017. <https://de.statista.com/statistik/daten/studie/631000/umfrage/endergebnis-der-us-praesidentschaftswahl-2016-nach-anzahl-der-wahlmaenner/>.

"Erweiterung Der Europäischen Union." *Die Bundesregierung.* N.p., 11 July 2014. Web. 13 Feb. 2017. <https://www.bundesregierung.de/Content/DE/StatischeSeiten/Breg/Europa/Artikel/2005-12-20-europa-dossier-erweiterung-der-europaeischen-union.html?nn=392696>.

Fehndrich, Martin. "US-Repräsentantenhaus." *Wahlrecht.* N.p., 06 Feb. 2004. Web. 13 Feb. 2017. <www.wahlrecht.de/ausland/house.html.>.

Fehndrich, Martin. "US-Senat." *Wahlrecht.* N.p., 06 Feb. 2004. Web. 12 Feb. 2017. <www.wahlrecht.de/ausland/senat.html.>.

Freidel, Frank, and Hugh Sidey. "George Washington." *White House.* N.p., 2006. Web. 10 Feb. 2017. <https://www.whitehouse.gov/1600/presidents/georgewashington>.

Freidel, Frank, and Hugh Sidey. "John Adams." *White House.* N.p., 2006. Web. 10 Feb. 2017. <https://www.whitehouse.gov/1600/presidents/johnadams>.

Fuchs, Hans Joachim. "Umwelt Und Nachhaltigkeit." *Konrad Adenauer Stiftung.* N.p., n.d. Web. 14 Feb. 2017. <http://www.kas.de/wf/de/71.7706/>.

"Funktion und Aufgabe." *Deutscher Bundestag.* N.p., 31 May 2013. Web. 31 Jan. 2017. <https://www.bundestag.de/parlament/aufgaben#url=L3BhcmxhbWVudC9hdWZnYWJlbi8xOTcxODY=&mod=mod454432>.

Gellner, Winand, and Martin Kleiber. "Der Senat." *Das Regierungssystem Der USA, Eine Einführung*. Baden-Baden: Nomos Verlagsgeselltschaft, 2012. 39-178. Print.

"Gemeinden/Kommunale Selbstverwaltung." *Bundeszentrale für politische Bildung*. N.p., n.d. Web. 29 Jan. 2017. <http://www.bpb.de/nachschlagen/lexika/handwoerterbuch-politisches-system/202028/gemeinden-kommunale-selbstverwaltung?p=all>.

"George Washington." *Lernhelfer*. N.p., 2010. Web. 14 Feb. 2017. <https://www.lernhelfer.de/schuelerlexikon/geschichte/artikel/george-washington>.

Gersch, Clemens. "Hintergrund: Die Macht des amerikanischen Präsidenten." *Planet Schule*. N.p., n.d. Web. 4 Feb. 2017. <https://www.planet-schule.de/wissenspool/usa-wahl/inhalt/hintergrund/die-macht-des-praesidenten.html>.

"Geschichte Der Vereinigten Staaten." *Wikipedia*. N.p., n.d. Web. 14 Feb. 2017. <https://de.wikipedia.org/wiki/Geschichte_der_Vereinigten_Staaten>.

"Gewaltenteilung - Politisches System Der USA." *Magazin USA.com*. N.p., n.d. Web. 4 Feb. 2017. <http://www.magazinusa.com/us/info/show.aspx?unit=politics&doc=2>.

"Gewaltenteilung." *Deutsch-werden.de*. N.p., 13 Nov. 2008. Web. 12 Feb. 2017. <http://www.deutsch-werden.de/gewaltenteilung-legislative-exekutive-judikative>.

Grünhagen, Jürgen. "Die Ölkrise 1973." *N-tv*. N.p., 25 Nov. 2009. Web. 14 Feb. 2017. <http://www.n-tv.de/politik/dossier/Deutschland-autofrei-article605647.html>.

Heinz, Tobias. "Wiederaufbau Durch Ausländer – Türken Und Türkische Gastarbeiter in Deutschland." *Formelheinz*. N.p., 08 Sept. 2009. Web. 14 Feb. 2017. <http://www.formelheinz.de/index.php/20090908274/Kultur/Wiederaufbau-in-Deutschland-Beitrag-der-Gastarbeiter.html>.

Hemmerich, Lisa. "Das Folgenreichste Versehen Der DDR-Geschichte." *Spiegel Online*. N.p., 09 Nov. 2009. Web. 7 Feb. 2017. <http://www.spiegel.de/politik/deutschland/schabowskis-legendaerer-auftritt-das-folgenreichste-versehen-der-ddr-geschichte-a-660203.html>.

Hesse, Joachim Jens, and Thomas Ellwein. "Das Deutsche Regierungssystem: Ausgangsbedingungen Und Entwicklung." *Das Regierungssytem Der Bundesrepublik Deutschland.* Berlin: De Gruyter Rechtswissenschaften Verlags GmbH, 2004.11-17 Print.

"Historische Entwicklung Und Entstehung Der 16 Bundesländer." *Deutschland Ueberblick.de.* N.p., n.d. Web. 14 Feb. 2017. <http://www.deutschland-ueberblick.de/bundeslaender/>.

Hoffmann, Lars. "Exekutive." *Americanet.* N.p., n.d. Web. 4 Feb. 2017. <http://www.americanet.de/html/politisches_system__executive.html>.

Hoffmann, Lars. "Judikative." *Americanet.* N.p., n.d. Web. 4 Feb. 2017. <http://www.americanet.de/html/politisches_system__judikative.html>.

Hoffmann, Lars. "Legislative." *Americanet.* N.p., n.d. Web. 4 Feb. 2017. <http://www.americanet.de/html/politisches_system__legislativ.html>.

Hoffmann, Lars. "Politisches System Der USA." *Americanet.* N.p., n.d. Web. 4 Feb. 2017. <http://www.americanet.de/politisches_system__ubersicht.html>.

Hofmann, Rebecca. "Entstehung Der Grünen." *Planet Wissen.* WDR, 22 June 2016. Web. 7 Feb. 2017. <http://www.planet-wissen.de/geschichte/deutsche_geschichte/entstehung_der_gruenen/>.

"Kanzleramt." *Die Bundeskanzlerin.* N.p., n.d. Web. 13 Feb. 2017. <https://www.bundeskanzlerin.de/Webs/BKin/DE/Kanzleramt/Zeitstrahl/Merkel/merkel_node.html;jsessionid=AAAD33070707BEAE2A64F31DB73F95E0.s3t1>

"Konföderierte Staaten Von Amerika." *Lexas.* N.p., n.d. Web. 14 Feb. 2017. <http://www.lexas.de/nordamerika/usa/geschichte/konfoederierte_staaten/>.

"Kongress - Fragmentierte Legislative." *Bundeszentrale Für Politische Bildung.* N.p., 06 Oct. 2008. Web. 4 Feb. 2017. <http://www.bpb.de/internationales/amerika/usa/10649/kongress?p=all>.

Korte, Karl-Rudolf. "Das Personalisierte Verhältniswahlrecht." *Bundeszentrale Für Politische Bidlung.* N.p., 20 May 2009. Web. 14 Feb. 2017. <http://www.bpb.de/politik/wahlen/bundestagswahlen/62524/personalisierte-verhaeltniswahl?p=all>.

Korte, Karl-Rudolf. *Wahlen in Deutschland.* Bonn: Bundeszentrale für politische Bildung, 2013. Print.

Krauel, Torsten. "Wo Geld Nach Freiheit Duftet." *Welt Am Sonntag* 15 Jan. 2017, 3rd ed.: 2-3. Print.

Kriwet, Hildegard. "Wirtschaftswunder." *Planet Wissen.* N.p., 13 Aug. 2014. Web. 14 Feb. 2017. <http://www.planet-wissen.de/geschichte/deutsche_geschichte/wirtschaftswunder/index.html>.

Küsters, Hanns Jürgen. "Gründung Der Bundesrepublik Deutschland 1949." *Konrad Adenauer.* N.p., n.d. Web. 10 Feb. 2017. <https://www.konrad-adenauer.de/stichworte/deutschlandpolitik/gruendung-der-bundesrepublik-deutschland-1949>.

"Land (Deutschland)." *Wikipedia.* N.p., n.d. Web. 29 Jan. 2017. < https://de.wikipedia.org/wiki/Land_(Deutschland)>.

"Landtag wählt Dr. Dietmar Woidke zum Ministerpäsidenten und Ministerriege der neuen Landesregierung vereidigt." *Landtag Brandenburg.* N.p., n.d. Web. 29 Jan. 2017. <https://www.landtag.brandenburg.de/de/aktuelles/bildergalerie_2015/bildergalerie_2014/landtag_waehlt_dr._dietmar_woidke_zum_ministerpraesidenten_und_ministerriege_der_neuen_landesregierung_vereidigt/673228>.

"Landtagswahlen-Wofür eigentlich?" *RP Online.* N.p., 02 Sept. 2004. Web. 29 Jan. 2017. < http://www.rp-online.de/politik/deutschland/landtagswahlen-wofuer-eigentlich-aid-1.1620144>.

Langels, Otto. "Für Ein Amerika Ohne Sklaverei." *Deutschlandfunk.* N.p., 18 Dec. 2015. Web. 14 Feb. 2017. <http://www.deutschlandfunk.de/13-zusatzartikel-der-us-verfassung-fuer-ein-amerika-ohne.871.de.html?dram:article_id=340100>.

Lösche, Peter. "Merkmale Der US-Präsidialdemokratie." *Wissen.de*. N.p., n.d. Web. 12 Feb. 2017. <http://www.wissen.de/merkmale-der-us-praesidialdemokratie>.

"Mehrheitswahlrecht: Das "Winner-takes-all"-Prinzip." *Zeit Online*. N.p., 09 Nov. 2016. Web. 14 Feb. 2017. <http://www.zeit.de/news/2016-11/08/wahlen-mehrheitswahlrechtdas-winner-takes-all-prinzip-08221203>.

"Mitglieder des Bundesrates." *Bundesrat*. N.p., n.d. Web. 31 Jan. 2017. <http://www.bundesrat.de/DE/bundesrat/mitglieder/mitglieder-node.html>.

Munk, Stephanie. "US-Wahl 2016: Die wichtigsten Fragen und Antworten." *Merkur*. N.p., 08 Nov. 2016. Web. 1 Feb. 2017. <https://www.merkur.de/politik/us-wahl-2016-datum-kandidaten-umfrage-prognose-ablauf-praesident-zr-6815185.html>.

"Oberster Gerichtshof Der Vereinigten Staaten." *Wikipedia*. N.p., n.d. Web. 5 Feb. 2017. <https://de.wikipedia.org/wiki/Oberster_Gerichtshof_der_Vereinigten_Staaten>.

"Oberster Gerichtshof Der Vereinigten Staaten." *Wissen.de*. N.p., n.d. Web. 5 Feb. 2017. <http://www.wissen.de/lexikon/oberster-gerichtshof-der-vereinigten-staaten>.

Oelker, Laura, and Sybille Klormann. "Wie wird der US-Präsident gewählt?" *Zeit Online*. N.p., 6. Nov. 2012. Web. 1 Feb. 2017. <http://www.focus.de/politik/ausland/us-wahlen-2016/>.

Oldopp, Birgit. *Das politische System der USA, Eine Einführung*. Wiesbaden: VS Verlag für Sozialwissenschaften/GWV Fachverlage GmbH, 2005. 15-159. Print.

"Parlamentarische Demokratie." *Bundeszentrale Für Politische Bildung*. N.p., n.d. Web. 12 Feb. 2017. <http://www.bpb.de/izpb/8374/parlamentarische-demokratie>.

"Parteien in den USA." *Landeszentrale Für Politische Bildung Baden-Württemberg*. N.p., n.d. Web. 7 Feb. 2017. <http://www.uswahl.lpb-bw.de/parteien_amerika.html>.

Pawlak, Britta. "USA-Vereinigte Staaten Von Amerika." *Helles Köpfchen.de*. N.p., n.d. Web. 4 Feb. 2017. <https://www.helles-koepfchen.de/artikel/340.html>.

Petschow, Annabelle. "Zwei-plus-Vier-Vertrag." *Lebendiges Museum Online*. Stiftung Haus Der Geschichte Der Bundesrepublik Deutschland, 29 Feb. 2016. Web. 7 Feb. 2017. <https://www.hdg.de/lemo/kapitel/deutsche-einheit/weg-zur-einheit/zwei-plus-vier-vertrag.html>.

"Politisches System Der Vereinigten Staaten." *Wikipedia*. N.p., n.d. Web. 5 Feb. 2017. <https://de.wikipedia.org/wiki/Politisches_System_der_Vereinigten_Staaten#Judikative>.

Pötzsch, Horst. "Aufgaben des Bundestages." *Bundeszentrale für politische Bildung*. N.p., 15 Dec. 2009. Web. 31 Jan. 2017. <http://www.bpb.de/politik/grundfragen/deutschedemokratie/39341/aufgaben-des-bundestages>.

"Präsidentin und Präsidium." *Bundesrat*. N.p., n.d. Web. 31 Jan. 2017. <http://www.bundesrat.de/DE/bundesrat/praesidium/praesidium-node.html>.

"Prinzip der Gewaltenteilung." *Der Bundestag*. N.p., n.d. Web. 31 Jan. 2017. <https://www.bundestag.de/parlament/aufgaben/rechtsgrundlagen/gewaltenteilung/246408>.

Prof. Dr. Lösche, Peter. "US-Föderalismus." *Bundeszentrale Für Politische Bildung*. N.p., 06 Oct. 2008. Web. 5 Feb. 2017. <http://www.bpb.de/internationales/amerika/usa/10653/us-foederalismus?p=all>.

Radler, Christian. "Land Der Zwei-Parteien Herrschaft." *Tagesschau.de*. N.p., 10 Mar. 2008. Web. 7 Feb. 2017. <https://www.tagesschau.de/ausland/meldung245842.html>.

"Rassentrennung Für Legal Erklärt." *Welt*. N.p., 19 Mar. 2010. Web. 14 Feb. 2017. <https://www.welt.de/iphone_app/historyapp/article6842047/Rassentrennung-fuer-legal-erklaert.html>.

"Repräsentantenhaus Der Vereinigten Staaten." *Wikipedia*. N.p., 06 July 2006. Web. 4 Feb. 2017. <https://de.wikipedia.org/wiki/Repr%C3%A4sentantenhaus_der_Vereinigten_Staaten>.

Schmid, Michael. "Vor 50 Jahren: Busboykott in Montgomery." *Lebenshaus Schwäbisch Alb*. N.p., 30 Nov. 2005. Web. 14 Feb. 2017. <http://www.lebenshaus-alb.de/magazin/003378.html>.

Schneider, Gerd, and Christiane Toyka-Seid. "Wahlbenachrichtigung." *Bundeszentrale Für Politische Bildung*. N.p., 2013. Web. 14 Feb. 2017. <http://www.bpb.de/nachschlagen/lexika/das-junge-politik-lexikon/161764/wahlbenachrichtigung>.

Schweitzer, Eva. ""Dann Werden Sie Es Mit Der Kugel Tun"." *Spiegel Online*. N.p., 14 Apr. 2015. Web. 14 Feb. 2017. <http://www.spiegel.de/einestages/attentat-auf-abraham-lincoln-verschwoerungstheorien-a-1028259.html>.

Seiffert, Jaenette. "Für das Volk-der deutsche Bundestag." *DW Made for minds*. N.p., 14 Oct. 2013. Web. 31 Jan. 2017. <http://www.dw.com/de/f%C3%BCr-das-volk-der-deutsche-bundestag/a-17038443>.

"Senat Der Vereinigten Staaten." *Wikipedia*. N.p., 29 June 2006. Web. 4 Feb. 2017. <https://de.wikipedia.org/wiki/Senat_der_Vereinigten_Staaten>.

"So funktionieren Wahlen: Allgemein, unmittelbar, frei, gleich und geheim." *Mach´s ab 16! in Brandenburg*. N.p., n.d. Web. 28 Jan. 2017. <http://www.machs-ab-16.de/waehlen-ab-16/so-funktionieren-wahlen-allgemein-unmittelbar-frei-gleich-und-geheim>.

Spörl, Gerhard. "Feldzug Der Friedliebenden." *Spiegel Online*. N.p., 17 Jan. 2014. Web. 14 Feb. 2017. <http://www.spiegel.de/einestages/erster-weltkrieg-kriegseintritt-amerikas-1917-unter-woodrow-wilson-a-953288.html>.

"Stellung der Kommunen im Staatsaufbau." *Niedersächsisches Ministerium für Inneres und Sport*. N.p., n.d. Web. 29 Jan. 2017. <http://www.mi.niedersachsen.de/themen/kommunen/stellung_kommunen_im_staatsaufbau/60388.html>.

Stevenson, Scot. "Amerikaner Wählen Alle Zwei Jahre." *N-TV*. N.p., 02 Nov. 2010. Web. 3 Feb. 2017. <http://www.n-tv.de/politik/Amerikaner-waehlen-alle-zwei-Jahre-article1840546.html>.

Stöver, Bernd. "Der Kalte Krieg Und Das Wettrüsten." *Bundeszentrale Für Politische Bildung*. N.p., 11 Oct. 2008. Web. 14 Feb. 2017. <http://www.bpb.de/internationales/amerika/usa/10614/kalter-krieg?p=all>.

Straaß, Johannes, and Gerhard Krahl, Prof. Dr. "Das Politische System in Deutschland." *Politische Bildung Schwaben*. N.p., 30 June 2013. Web. 29 Jan. 2017. < http://www.politische-bildung-schwaben.net/2013/06/das-politische-system-in-deutschland/>.

Strutynski, Peter. "Warum Es Noch Kein Impeachment-Verfahren Gegen US-Präsident George W. Bush Gibt." *AG Friedensforschung*. N.p., n.d. Web. 4 Feb. 2017. <http://www.agfriedensforschung.de/regionen/USA/impeachment.html>.

Thurich, Eckart. "Bundesregierung." *Bundeszentrale Für Politische Bildung*. N.p., 2011. Web. 13 Feb. 2017. <http://www.bpb.de/nachschlagen/lexika/pocketpolitik/16360/bundesregierung>.

"Trump Will Obersten Richter Am Dienstag Benennen." *Zeit Online*. N.p., 30 Jan. 2017. Web. 14 Feb. 2017. <http://www.zeit.de/politik/ausland/2017-01/supreme-court-donald-trump-richter-kandidat>.

"United States Senate." *United States Senate*. N.p., n.d. Web. 4 Feb. 2017. <https://www.senate.gov/>.

"US-Geschichte Der Zweite Weltkrieg." *About the USA*. N.p., Apr. 2008. Web. 14 Feb. 2017. <https://usa.usembassy.de/geschichte-ww2.htm>.

"US-Wahlen 2016." *Focus Online*. N.p., 04 May 2016. Web. 1 Feb. 2017. <http://www.focus.de/politik/ausland/us-wahlen-2016/>.

"Verfassungen Der Vereinigten Staaten Von Amerika." *Verfassungen.net*. N.p., 16 Feb. 2006. Web. 14 Feb. 2017. <http://www.verfassungen.net/us/verf87-i.htm>.

"Wahl der Abgeordneten und Mandatsverteilung." *Deutscher Bundestag*. N.p., n.d. Web. 28 Jan. 2017. <https://www.bundestag.de/parlament/wahlen/abg_wahl/245234>.

"Wahlbeteiligung Bei Bundestagswahlen." *Bundestagswahl 2017*. N.p., n.d. Web. 14 Feb. 2017. <https://bundestagswahl-2017.com/wahlbeteiligung/>.

"Wahlen, Hintergrund: Senat Und Repräsentantenhaus Im US-Kongress." *Focus Online*. N.p., 03 Nov. 2010. Web. 4 Feb. 2017. <http://www.focus.de/politik/deutschland/wahlen-hintergrund-senat-und-repraesentantenhaus-im-us-kongress_aid_568431.html>.

"Wahlfunktion." *Landtag von Baden-Württemberg*. N.p., n.d. Web. 29 Jan. 2017. <https://www.landtagbw.de/home/derlandtag/parlament/wahlfunktion.html>.

"Wahlrecht Für Afro-Amerikaner." *Was Ist Was*. N.p., 03 Aug. 2005. Web. 14 Feb. 2017. <http://www.wasistwas.de/archiv-geschichte-details/wahlrecht-fuer-afro-amerikaner.html>.

"Wahlrecht Für Frauen." *Berliner Zeitung*. N.p., 26 Aug. 1995. Web. 14 Feb. 2017. <http://www.berliner-zeitung.de/wahlrecht-fuer-frauen-der-usa-16886236>.

"Wahlrecht." *Rechtslexikon.net*. N.p., n.d. Web. 27 Jan. 2017. <http://www.rechtslexikon.net/d/wahlrecht/wahlrecht.htm>.

"Was die Aufgaben der Kommunen sind." *Land Brandenburg*. N.p., n.d. Web. 29 Jan. 2017. <http://www.kinderleicht.brandenburg.de/cms/detail.php/bb1.c.301100.de>.

"Was ist Föderalismus?" *Was ist Föderalismus?* N.p., n.d. Web. 29 Jan. 2017. < http://europe.hkbu.edu.hk/polshyp/bland/bland5.htm>.

"Washington (dpa) - In Den USA Gibt Es Im Wesentlichen Zwei Große Konkurrierende Parteien:." *Web.de*. N.p., 05 Nov. 2014. Web. 7 Feb. 2017. <https://web.de/magazine/politik/kongresswahl-barack-obama/hintergrund-republikaner-demokraten-30188620>.

"Weißes Haus in Washington." *Washington-reise.de*. N.p., n.d. Web. 5 Feb. 2017. <http://www.washington-reise.de/weisses-haus.htm>.

"Welche Wahlen gibt es?" *Einmischen, Mitmischen. Politik für alle!* N.p., n.d. Web. 27 Jan. 2017. <http://sonderpaedagoge.de/mitmischen/index.php?menuid=34>.

"Wie Hoch War Die Wahlbeteiligung Bei Den US-Wahlen 2016?" *Landeszentrale Für Politische Bildung Vaden-Württemberg.* N.p., 20 Dec. 2016. Web. 14 Feb. 2017. <http://www.uswahl.lpb-bw.de/wahlverhalten_grafik.html>.

Würz, Markus. "Alliierte Besatzung." *Lebendiges Museum Online.* Stiftung Haus Der Geschichte Der Bundesrepublik Deutschland, 22 Feb. 2016. Web. 7 Feb. 2017. <https://www.hdg.de/lemo/kapitel/nachkriegsjahre/befreiung-und-besatzung/alliierte-besatzung.html>.

Würz, Markus. "Geteiltes Deutschland." *Lebendiges Museum Deutschland.* Stiftung Haus Der Geschichte Der Bundesrepublik Deutschland, 27 Oct. 2014. Web. 14 Feb. 2017. <https://www.hdg.de/lemo/kapitel/geteiltes-deutschland>.

Zicht, Wilko. "Ergebnisse Der Bundestagswahlen." *Wahlrecht.* N.p., 27 Oct. 2013. Web. 7 Feb. 2017. <http:p//www.wahlrecht.de/ergebnisse/bundestag.htm>.

Zicht, Wilko. "Komunalwahlrecht." *Wahlrecht.* N.p., 1999. Web. 28 Jan. 2017. <http://www.wahlrecht.de/kommunal/niedersachsen.html>.

Zicht, Wilko. "Landtagswahlrecht." *Wahlrecht.* N.p., 1999. Web. 27 Jan. 2017. <http://www.wahlrecht.de/landtage/>.

YOUR KNOWLEDGE HAS VALUE

- We will publish your bachelor's and master's thesis, essays and papers

- Your own eBook and book - sold worldwide in all relevant shops

- Earn money with each sale

Upload your text at www.GRIN.com and publish for free